Colorful Creations
Positively Inspired

Jess Volinski

DESIGN ORIGINALS
an Imprint of Fox Chapel Publishing
www.d-originals.com

Be Yourself to Be Creative

The thing I love most about art—making it myself or enjoying others' creations—is that **art allows you to be yourself by expressing yourself.** Whatever you love, whatever is important to you, whatever makes you who you are should come out in your art. By making art that matters to you, you're starting a conversation with everyone who sees it. You're saying, "Hey! This matters to me. What do **you** think about it?"

You might be wondering, how exactly do I express myself with art? That's where the **Elements of Art** come in. You might remember these from art class. Just like writers use words to tell a story, artists use these visual elements to express themselves and start their art conversation. All visual art—whether it is a painting in a museum, storyboards for a movie, a pattern on a bag, or a coloring book page—uses some combination of these seven basic building blocks of art. Not all art has to include all seven elements, but most art will include a few.

The Elements of Art

A **line** is formed as the connected distance between two points. Lines can be thick or thin, straight or curved.

Space refers to the areas in a piece of art that are around or within different parts of the art. There are two kinds of space: negative (space around areas), and positive (space within areas).

A **shape** is a defined area of space—a circle, square, blob, or a flower petal are all shapes.

Texture refers to the way the art physically feels when touched, or how an artist visually makes the art **look** like it would feel. Shading with pencils is an example of this type of visual texture.

Something has **form** if it has volume (or creates the illusion of volume). A three-dimensional sculpture has form. A two-dimensional drawing with shading that makes it appear three-dimensional can also have form.

Color is created when light hits an object and is reflected to our eyes. A color can be described with three properties: hue (the color's name, such as "red"), value (how light or dark the color is, also called a tint or shade of the color), and intensity (how vivid or dull the color is).

Value refers to the relationship between light areas and dark areas in a piece of art.

Let's look at one of my drawings and see what Elements of Art are here. Even though this is just a simple black and white drawing, it has line, shape, and space. When you color it, you'll probably add form, color, value, and maybe even texture. That's all seven Elements of Art.

Shape

Line

Space (negative): The shape inside the loop is a negative space.

Space (positive): The shape of this leaf creates a positive space.

Form (and texture): The colored pencil texture makes the flower look three-dimensional, giving it form.

Value (light)

Texture

Value (dark)

Color

SHE Believed SHE COULD SO SHE DID

Get Inspired by Color

When it comes to expressing emotion, I think color is probably the most powerful Element of Art. To me, there's no better way to express how you're feeling, or how you want someone else to feel, than through the use of color. Just think of some of your favorite memories and how they make you feel. I bet color plays a big part of what you remember. Whether it's a beautiful sunset, the green of spring after a long, cold winter, or a perfectly clean, white expanse of snow, color makes a huge impact on us, both visually and emotionally. Just look at the way different colors can give the same flower drawing a completely different feel.

I've found that planning is key when working with color. If you're like me and you just **love** color, it might seem a bit overwhelming to get started. There are just so many color choices! And it's easy to fall into the rut of using the same colors over and over again, just because you like them. Making color decisions before you start can make you feel comfortable using new colors. Plus, you won't have to make a choice when you're in the midst of coloring and decide you don't like the result as much as you thought you would. A great way to try some new color combinations is to take a few minutes—it won't take long!—to create your own palettes before you get started.

Here's a fun trick I've learned for making palettes. It works especially well if you're using markers or colored pencils. Lay out all of your markers (or pencils) on a table or floor so you can see every single color you have. Pick one favorite marker (pencil) that will serve as the **anchor color** for your palette. Make it a color you really enjoy working with (or for a challenge, maybe a color you never work with). Now, pick two or three other markers (pencils) that complement your anchor color and place those next to your anchor color to start building a palette. Keep going until you have picked five or six colors. At this point, you don't even have to use them— you're just putting them side-by-side to see how the colors look together. Keep adding or switching colors until you like what you see. It's so easy to swap different colors in and out this way. Once you have a group of colors that you like, test them out on paper to make sure you still like the way they look together. If you love it, be sure to create a sample page with the names of the markers/colors you used so you won't forget. This is a great way to quickly create a whole library of color palettes for yourself.

Another great place to get color inspiration is literally from the world around you. Color is everywhere—your clothing, your bag, even a tissue box—there are probably patterns and designs with interesting color palettes surrounding you now! I'm sure there are things you bought because you liked the colors, so use those things that you love as inspiration. I once bought a pack of hair elastics simply because they had the most beautiful combination of blues and purples. Almost anything, anywhere, can become a color inspiration, so always keep your eyes open!

A Spectrum of Emotion

Color can be a great way to express yourself and define your mood. When you sit down to color, ask yourself, "How do I feel today? How can I use color to express that feeling?" Sometimes you might even feel something you can't quite put into words, but you can express it with color.

I've included some of my favorite palettes below. Each one is paired with the emotion that best describes how the color combination makes me feel. But keep in mind that everyone is different, and that's what makes art so exciting. I love to use bright colors, but maybe you like more subdued colors. My "relaxed" palette might be your "cozy." There is no right or wrong when it comes to color! Use these palettes as a starting point and see how they make you feel. Try adding or taking away

a color to customize the palette to reflect your taste and style. Then, make your own page full of YOUR favorite color palettes!

The next few pages contain some colored examples. On each page, I've included a palette with each individual color that was used, shown separately, so you can easily match your marker, pencil, or paint colors to the colors used in the design.

Whether you use one of my palettes or create your own, always be sure the colors you choose reflect who you are and how you're feeling.

Now go gather up your art supplies—it's time to color!

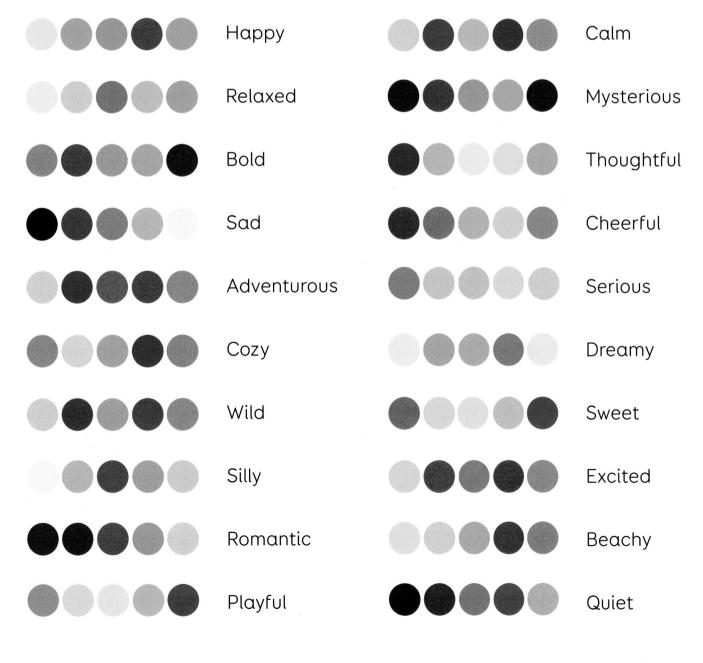

Happy

Relaxed

Bold

Sad

Adventurous

Cozy

Wild

Silly

Romantic

Playful

Calm

Mysterious

Thoughtful

Cheerful

Serious

Dreamy

Sweet

Excited

Beachy

Quiet

Take the Color Wheel for a Spin

A lot of times, simply following your feelings will lead you right to your color choices, but sometimes you might get stuck, and that's OK! Maybe you just don't know what you're feeling or you want to try something different with color and aren't sure where to start. The color wheel can be an awesome guide to help you make color choices.

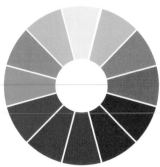

The Color Wheel

The color wheel is a visual guide to the relationships between colors based on their position on the wheel. When placed together, certain colors look harmonious while others might clash. It all depends on the relationship of the colors to one another. Each color in a palette needs to be surrounded by the right companions to shine!

The color wheel diagrams below are a great starting place to find colors that will automatically look lovely together. But always remember, the color wheel is only a guide. Feel free to add more colors to a palette or take some away. The best color choices are always the ones that reflect how you're feeling and what makes you happy. Have fun!

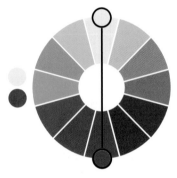

Complementary Colors
Complementary colors are pairs of opposites. They are directly across from one another on the color wheel.

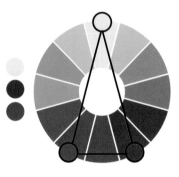

Split Complementary Colors
A split complementary color palette is created when one color is grouped with the two colors on either side of its complementary color.

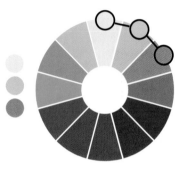

Analogous Colors
Analogous color palettes are created by choosing several colors that sit right next to each other on the color wheel.

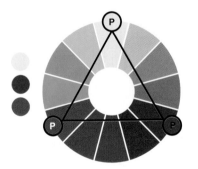

Primary Triadic Colors
Triadic means "group of three." The three primary colors (red, yellow, and blue) form a triadic palette when grouped together.

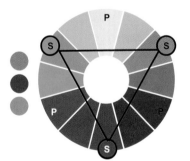

Secondary Triadic Colors
Secondary colors are the colors directly in between the primary colors on the color wheel. When you shift the triangle around the wheel by two spaces, you've found the secondary colors.

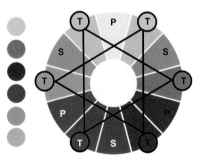

Tertiary Colors
Tertiary colors fall in between the primary and secondary colors. These are some of my favorite colors to work with!

Tetradic Colors
Tetradic means "group of four." Using a rectangle or square to choose colors on the color wheel is a fun way to instantly create a group of four colors that look great together. Both use two sets of complementary colors. Try rotating the rectangle or square around the wheel to create many different palettes.

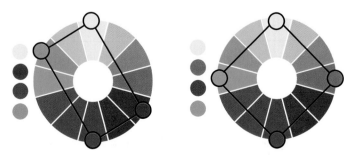

Markers (Tombow), colored pencils (Prismacolor). Color by Jess Volinski. Today Is a Happy Day, page 57.

Colored pencils (Prismacolor, Faber-Castell). Color by Lynette Parmenter. Follow Your Dreams, page 61.

Colored pencils (Prismacolor). Color by Keara Irby. Love Grows Here, page 59.

Markers (Sharpie), gel pens. Color by Roslyn Coronado. *Everything Is Going to Be OK*, page 41.

Markers (Sharpie, Copic, Bic), colored pencils (Prismacolor), gel pens. Color by Keara Irby. Choose Joy, page 79.

Markers (Sharpie), gel pens, pens, colored pencils. Color by Roslyn Coronado. Bloom Where You Are Planted, page 49.

Colored pencils (Prismacolor). Color by Darla Tjelmeland. Embrace Change, page 35.

Colored pencils (Prismacolor), gel pens (Uni-Ball Signo). Color by Keara Irby. Hope, Faith, Love, page 77.

Colored pencils (Prismacolor). Color by Darla Tjelmeland. She Believed, page 31.

Colored pencils (Prismacolor, Faber–Castell). Color by Lynette Parmenter. Listen to Your Heart, page 53.

Choose **three colors** that are equally spaced from one another, making a triangle on the color wheel to create your own **triadic** color palettes!

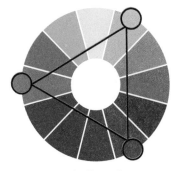

Triadic colors

Palette examples

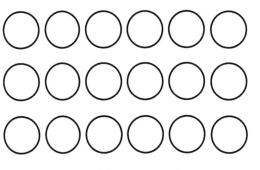

Make your own!
Also try adding a few additional colors.

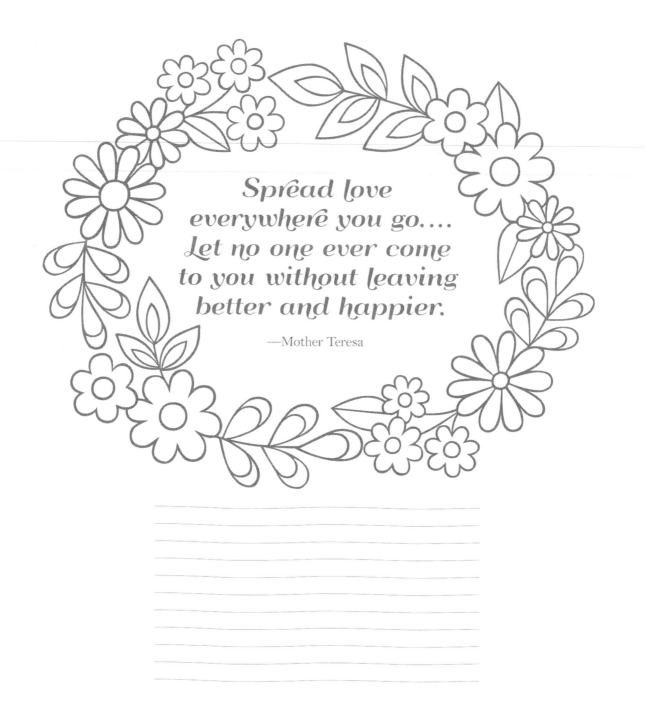

Spread love
everywhere you go....
Let no one ever come
to you without leaving
better and happier.
—Mother Teresa

Kindness Matters

Try choosing a palette of **3, 4, or 5 colors** that are right next to each other on the color wheel to make your own analogous color palettes!

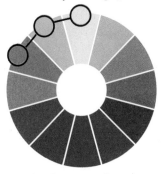

Analogous colors

Palette examples

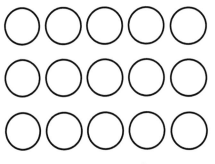

Make your own!
Also try adding a few additional colors.

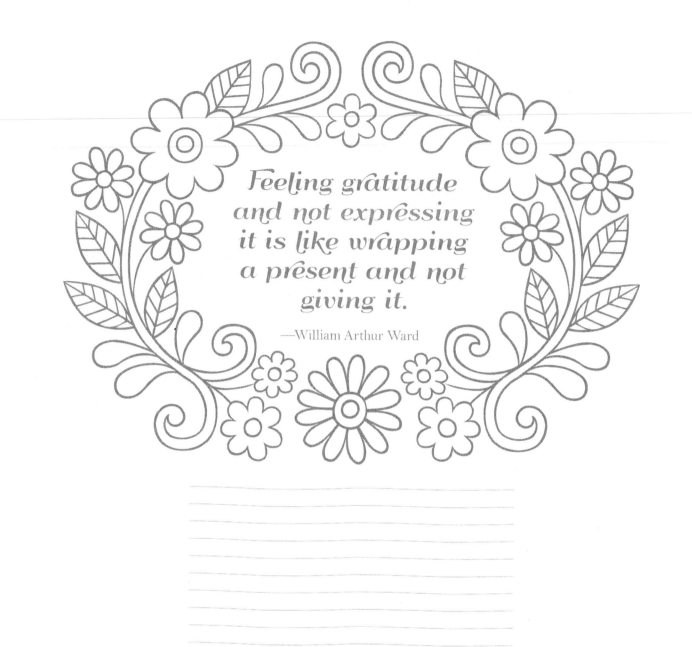

Feeling gratitude
and not expressing
it is like wrapping
a present and not
giving it.

—William Arthur Ward

Give Thanks

Choose **four** colors that are equally spaced around the color wheel in a **square** to make your own **tetradic** color palette!

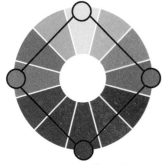

Square tetradic colors

Palette examples

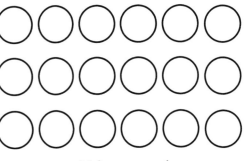

Make your own!
Also try adding a few additional colors.

It is not how much
we have, but how
much we enjoy, that
makes happiness.

—Charles Spurgeon

Live Simply

Find a color you like and then choose the two colors right next to that color's complement to make your own **split complementary** color palette!

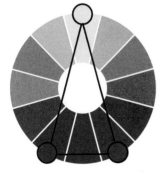

Split complementary colors

Palette examples

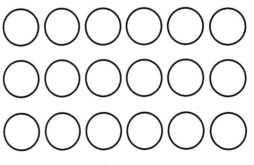

Make your own!
Also try adding a few additional colors.

Very little is needed to
make a happy life.

—Marcus Aurelius

Relax and Let Go

Choose four colors that are spaced around the color wheel in a **rectangle** to make your own **tetradic** color palette!

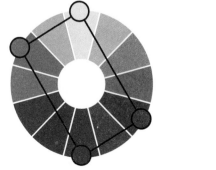

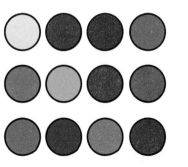

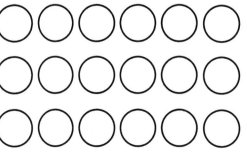

Rectangle tetradic colors

Palette examples

Make your own!
Also try adding a few additional colors.

It's a good day for
a good day.

—Unknown

Life Is a Gift

EVERY Day IS A NEW BEGINNING

Happiness is
not out there,
it's in you.

—Unknown

New Beginning

JUST Breathe

This is a wonderful day.
I've never seen this
one before.

—Maya Angelou

_____

Just Breathe

Attitude is a little thing that makes a big difference.

—Unknown

_____
_____
_____
_____
_____
_____
_____
_____
_____

33

They may forget what you said—but they will never forget how you made them feel.

—Carl W. Buehner

Always Look Up

EMBRACE Change

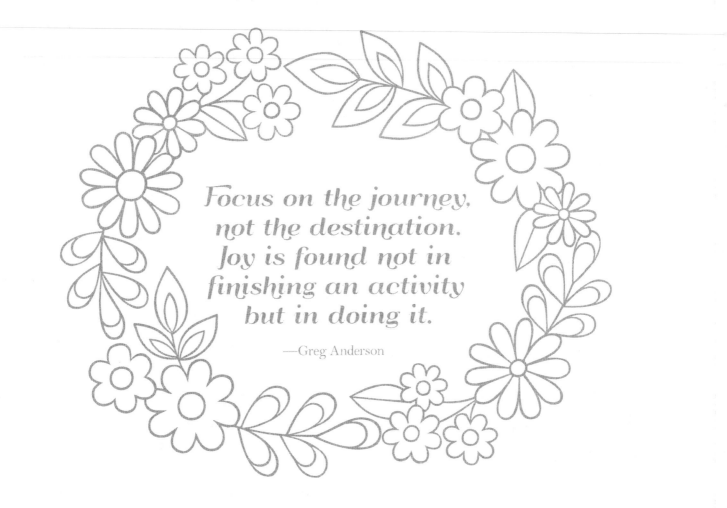

Focus on the journey,
not the destination.
Joy is found not in
finishing an activity
but in doing it.

—Greg Anderson

Embrace Change

Be Happy Now

Happiness is not something ready made. It comes from your own actions.

—Dalai Lama

Be Happy Now

Joy in looking and
comprehending
is nature's most
beautiful gift.

—Albert Einstein

Things turn out best for people who make the best of the way things turn out.

—Unknown

Everything Is Going to Be OK

No matter where you are on your journey, that's exactly where you need to be. The next road is always ahead.

—Oprah Winfrey

Hope

My HAPPY LIST

The most important thing is to enjoy your life—to be happy—it's all that matters.

—Audrey Hepburn

Happy List

Sometimes your joy is the source of your smile, but sometimes your smile can be the source of your joy.

—Thich Nhat Hanh

Follow your bliss and don't be afraid, and doors will open where you didn't know they were going to be.

—Joseph Campbell

Listen to Your Heart

ENJOY this Moment

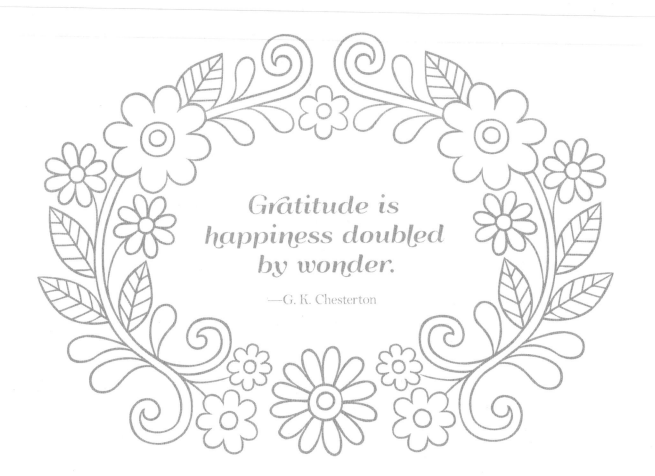

Gratitude is happiness doubled by wonder.

—G. K. Chesterton

Whoever is happy
will make others
happy, too.

—Anne Frank

_____
_____
_____
_____
_____
_____
_____
_____
_____
_____

Today Is a Happy Day

Love Grows Here

Love is that condition in which the happiness of another person is essential to your own.

—Robert A. Heinlein

Love Grows Here

FOLLOW *your* DREAMS

May your choices
reflect your hopes,
not your fears.

—Nelson Mandela

Follow Your Dreams

He is a wise man who does not grieve for the things which he has not, but rejoices for those which he has.

—Epictetus

Stay Strong

Positive anything
is better than
negative nothing.

—Elbert Hubbard

Keep Going

Everything is a gift of the universe—even joy, anger, jealousy, frustration, or separateness. Everything is perfect either for our growth or our enjoyment.

—Ken Keyes Jr.

_____
_____
_____
_____
_____
_____
_____
_____

Great Things

Live LIFE FULL OF Joy AND WONDER

Those who don't
believe in magic will
never find it.

—Roald Dahl

_____
_____
_____
_____
_____
_____
_____

Joy and Wonder

I AM Grateful FOR

There is always
so much to be
thankful for.

—Unknown

Being Grateful

Be Still

Appreciation is
a wonderful thing.
It makes what is
excellent in others
belong to us as well.

—Voltaire

Keep your face to
the sunshine and
you cannot see
a shadow.

—Helen Keller

_____
_____
_____
_____
_____
_____
_____
_____
_____

Hope, Faith, Love